AUSTRALIAN

LABRADOODLE DOG

A Complete Dog Training Guide

An Expert Guide To The Grooming, Commands, Care, Exercises, Feeding, Whelping, Health Issues, Lifespan And Much More

Dezi Drogo

Table of Contents

CHAPTER ONE

The Origins And History Of The Australian Labradoodle Dog

The 1980s marked the beginning of the relatively recent history of the Australian Labradoodle dog breed.

It was first created in Australia as a hybrid between the Labrador Retriever and the Standard Poodle to produce a sociable, hypoallergenic service dog.

Wally Conron of the Royal Guide Dogs Association of Australia started the breeding program to create guide dogs that would be appropriate for persons who have allergies to canine hair.

Further crossings were undertaken to attain uniformity in features like coat texture and temperament after the first crossbreeding efforts produced Labradoodles with a variety of coat kinds and sizes.

Later, other breeds were developed to improve certain traits, including the English and American Cocker Spaniel.

The outcome was a versatile and very trainable dog with the gentle and sociable traits of the Labrador Retriever with the intellect and trainability of the Poodle.

Due to its hypoallergenic hair and lovable personality, the Australian Labradoodle has become popular both as a service dog and as a family companion. Today, they are respected for their intellect, adaptability, and friendly temperament and are recognized as a distinct breed by several kennel groups.

The Australian Labradoodle's Physical Characteristics

Australian Labradoodles are a breed renowned for their endearing physical features. The bodies of these dogs are often strong and proportionate, giving them an athletic aspect. Depending on the size variance, they may range in height at the shoulder from 14 to 24 inches (35 to 60 cm) and have a medium-sized physique. One of an Australian Labradoodle's most distinctive characteristics is its coat. It is good for those with sensitivities since it is often thick, wavy, and allergy-friendly.

In addition to cream, chocolate, black, apricot, caramel, and silver, the coat may also be found in other hues. Usually broad and rounded, their expressive eyes exude warmth and intellect. Australian Labradoodles have long, drooping ears that perfectly frame their lovely faces. They have a warm, happy countenance that belies their social, lively disposition. Australian Labradoodles are loved wherever they go because of their attractive physical characteristics.

The Behavior And Character Of The Australian Labradoodle Dog

The Australian Labradoodle is a favored breed among many dog lovers because of its sweet disposition and endearing demeanor. This breed displays a variety of amazing attributes as a result of the traits it inherited from its Labrador Retriever,

Poodle, and Cocker Spaniel parent breeds.

Australian Labradoodles are often characterized as loving and friendly. They naturally have the propensity to build intimate bonds with their owners, developing enduring relationships and turning into devoted pals.

They are a great option for families or houses with many pets since they are quite friendly and like the company of both people and other animals.

Australian Labradoodles are kind, clever, and eager to please, which makes them very trainable. They are adept at a variety of tasks, including therapeutic work, agility training, and obedience. Their capacity to readily adapt to many settings and lifestyles is another factor in their adaptability.

Additionally, Australian Labradoodles are renowned for being lively. They have a happy spirit that keeps them interested and energetic, which makes them excellent playmates and partners for outdoor activities.

Overall, the temperament and demeanor of the Australian Labradoodle combine to produce a delightful, amiable, and wise companion that enriches the lives of its owners.

CHAPTER TWO

The Australian Labradoodle's Physical Characteristics

The medium-sized Australian Labradoodle dog breed is distinguished by its distinctive physical features. These dogs often have a physique that is well-balanced and strong.

They have a square-shaped skull and expressive, medium-sized, widely-spaced almond-shaped eyes. The Labradoodle's floppy, close-to-the-head ears contribute to its adorable look.

The coat of the Australian Labradoodle is one of its distinguishing characteristics. These dogs have a hypoallergenic, non-shedding coat that has different textures, such as wavy, curly, or straight.

Their coat may be dense and thick, offering insulation and weather protection. Australian Labradoodles may be found in a variety of hues, including parti (a mix of colors), cream, chocolate, caramel, and black.

Australian Labradoodles may range in size based on their breeding and history. They typically weigh between 30 and 65 pounds (14-29 kg) and stand between 17 and 24 inches (43-61 cm) at the shoulder. Overall, the Australian Labradoodle's physical traits add to its attractiveness and make them a desirable option for dog lovers looking for a cuddly and low-shedding companion.

Similarities And Differences Between Australian Labradoodle Dogs

The intelligent, amiable, and hypoallergenic Australian Labradoodle is a well-liked and adaptable breed. Australian Labradoodles and Labradoodles in general have several distinguishing characteristics that set them apart and together.

The genesis of each is a significant distinction. The first Australian Labradoodles were developed in the late 1980s to produce a hypoallergenic service dog.

They are a hybrid of the Labrador Retriever, Poodle, and many additional breeds, including the Irish Water Spaniel and English Cocker Spaniel. As a mix between Labrador Retrievers and Poodles, Labradoodles were created in the 1970s.

Both breeds have comparable physical attributes that are shared by both in terms of appearance, such as a medium-sized, athletic physique and a wavy or curly coat. The gene pool of Australian

Labradoodles tends to be larger, and as a result, they may display a greater range of coat types, sizes, and colors.

Both breeds are renowned for their amiable, gregarious, and clever personalities when it comes to disposition. They often get along well with kids and are wonderful family pets. Both breeds must have consistent physical activity and mental stimulation to flourish.

Overall, the Australian Labradoodle and Labradoodle have many similarities, especially in terms of their disposition and appropriateness as family pets, despite minor distinctions in origin and coat variety.

How To Take Care Of An Australian Labradoodle

A well-liked breed, the Australian Labradoodle is renowned for its intelligence, friendliness, and low-shedding coat.

The health and well-being of these adorable canines depend on proper upkeep and care. Here are some crucial things to remember:

The most important thing is to groom yourself regularly. The distinctive coat of Australian Labradoodles has to be brushed at least once a week to avoid matting and tangling.

It is also advised to get monthly professional grooming treatments to keep their coats looking healthy.

For Australian Labradoodles, exercise is essential. These dogs need frequent walks, playing, and mental stimulation to be happy and healthy since they are so active and vivacious.

You may help them meet their demand for exercise by including them in games like fetch or agility training.

For you to stay healthy, you need to eat well. It is advised to feed dogs a balanced diet made up of premium dog food that is appropriate for their size and age.

For particular nutritional advice, speak with your veterinarian.

Australian Labradoodles need frequent veterinarian

examinations. For them to stay healthy, regular vaccines, parasite control, dental treatment, and general health examinations are required.

For Australian Labradoodles, socialization is important. To encourage their well-rounded growth and avert behavioral problems, expose them to a variety of situations, people, and animals from an early age.

Last but not least, provide your Australian Labradoodle with a nurturing and engaging environment. They like company, so spend time with them, provide them with interesting toys to keep their minds engaged, and make sure their home is cozy and secure.

You can give your Australian Labradoodle a happy, healthy, and meaningful life as a beloved part of your family by according to these care and upkeep instructions.

CHAPTER THREE

Australian Labradoodle Dog Nutrition And Feeding

The health and well-being of Australian Labradoodle dogs are significantly influenced by diet and feeding. These clever, athletic dogs need a balanced diet to support their busy lifestyle and keep their health at its best.

High-quality commercial dog food designed for medium to large breeds is often advised when feeding an Australian Labradoodle. In addition to actual meat as the main component, choose a brand that has a balanced ratio of carbs, healthy fats, vitamins, and minerals. Eat less food that has artificial fillers, additives, or byproducts.

Your Australian Labradoodle's age, size, activity level, and metabolism will all affect how much food you give them.

The proper serving size for your dog should be determined in consultation with your veterinarian. Compared to adult dogs, puppies often need smaller, more frequent meals.

Australian Labradoodles benefit from frequent exercise to avoid obesity and maintain their muscles toned in addition to a wholesome diet. Ensure that you give them plenty of chances to exercise, such as regular walks, playing, and cerebral stimulation.

Make sure your Australian Labradoodle always has access to clean, fresh water since proper hydration is also essential.

Last but not least, keep an eye on your dog's weight and overall health. Consult your veterinarian if you observe any noticeable changes in your pet's appetite, weight, or general health so they may be treated for any possible nutritional problems.

Your Australian Labradoodle will stay healthy, active, and content for years to come if you provide them with a balanced diet and address their nutritional requirements.

Activities And Exercises Of Australian Labradoodle Dog

The Australian Labradoodle is a lively, intelligent breed that enjoys exercise and physical activities. To maintain their happiness, health, and good behavior, regular exercise is necessary.

Given that these dogs have a medium to high level of energy, regular exercise is essential to keeping them from becoming bored and acting out destructively. Australian Labradoodles may benefit from a range of athletic activities. Long strolls or jogs are excellent for letting off steam and keeping their bodies in shape. They also like playing interactive activities like fetch or frisbee, which not only help them exercise physically but also sharpen their minds.

Another pastime that Australian Labradoodles are excellent at is swimming. Swimming is a terrific kind of exercise for them since they have a natural love for the water and maybe outstanding swimmers, particularly during the hot summer months.

Agility training may also be quite pleasant and advantageous for this breed. They pick things up quickly thanks to their intelligence and athleticism, and they are excellent at agility drills like obstacle courses and jumps.

It's vital to remember that each Australian Labradoodle will have different exercise requirements based on their age, health, and general level of activity. The health and happiness of this lovely breed are maintained by regular physical activity and exercise.

The Care For An Australian Labradoodle Dog's Coat And Grooming

An Australian Labradoodle dog's health and attractiveness depend on proper grooming and coat maintenance. With their plush, hypoallergenic coat, they may look and feel their best with the correct maintenance techniques.

To avoid matting and tangling of the Labradoodle's curly or wavy coat, regular brushing is essential. If there are any knots or tangles, they may be carefully removed with a wide-toothed comb or a slicker brush. The coat should be brushed at least twice or three times every week.

To prevent skin irritation, bathing should be done every four to six weeks using a gentle dog shampoo. It is best to give the coat a good brushing before washing to get rid of any loose hair and dirt. The grooming regimen should also include frequent tooth brushing, nail trimming, and ear cleaning.

Every few months, professional grooming appointments may assist to maintain the ideal look and make sure the coat is appropriately clipped to avoid matting or excessive length.

In addition to maintaining the Australian Labradoodle's gorgeous coat, proper grooming also encourages healthy skin and may assist spot any possible health problems.

CHAPTER FOUR

Australian Labradoodle Dog's Health Concerns And Common Medical Issues

Australian Labradoodles have a low prevalence of hereditary diseases and are typically healthy dogs. Like other dog breeds, they are susceptible to certain health disorders and widespread medical conditions.

To protect their dog's well-being, Labradoodle owners must be aware of these possible issues and take the necessary action.

Hip and elbow dysplasia, or the improper growth of these joints, is one of the main health issues in Labradoodles. Mobility problems and lameness may result from this disorder. A veterinarian's routine examinations and screenings may help spot and treat these orthopedic issues.

Another typical medical condition in Australian Labradoodles is allergies. They may be susceptible to both food allergies and environmental allergies (such as those caused by pollen or dust mites).

Excessive scratching, redness, and skin irritations are possible symptoms. These allergies may be relieved by working closely with a veterinarian, establishing a proper diet, and making changes to the surroundings.

Labradoodles may also be prone to eye conditions such as cataracts and progressive retinal atrophy (PRA). Early identification and adequate treatment may be aided by routine eye exams and monitoring.

In addition, Labradoodles may develop dental problems such as tartar accumulation, gum disease, and tooth rot, much like many other dog breeds. Maintaining excellent oral hygiene requires regular dental care, which includes brushing your teeth and getting your teeth cleaned by a professional.

Overall, proper breeding procedures, routine veterinarian care, a balanced diet, and enough exercise may greatly benefit Australian Labradoodles' health and well-being and help them have happy, meaningful lives.

Vaccinations For Australian Labradoodle Dogs And Preventive Care

A vital part of protecting the health and well-being of Australian Labradoodles is vaccination and preventative care. These witty and sociable dogs need to be properly immunized to guard against many viral illnesses. Puppy vaccinations normally start at 6 to 8 weeks of age and continue throughout the puppy's life.

Essential shots for Australian Labradoodles include rabies, hepatitis, parvovirus, and distemper vaccines. Additionally, dependent on their lifestyle and environment, they could get non-core vaccinations like leptospirosis or kennel cough defense.

Annual or biannual veterinarian checkups, which include thorough physical exams, parasite treatment, and dental care, are part of routine preventative care for Labradoodles. As required, routine blood tests and vaccines are given. To keep these dogs healthy, a correct food, exercise program, and grooming schedule must be followed.

To build a personalized vaccine and preventative care plan catered to their Australian Labradoodle's specific requirements, pet owners should speak with their veterinarian. Australian Labradoodle owners may contribute to the long, happy, and healthy lives of their dogs by being proactive and attentive in administering immunizations and preventative care.

CHAPTER FIVE

The Socialization And Training Of An Australian Labradoodle Puppy

An Australian Labradoodle dog's general behavior and well-being depend heavily on their training and socialization. To become polite and obedient companions, these social and clever dogs need constant training.

Early on in a Labradoodle's life, training should begin using positive reinforcement methods like praise and rewards. Sit, remain, and come are basic instructions that should be taught gradually, building on each achievement. Crate training is also advised to provide the dog with a secure and cozy environment.

To guarantee that Australian Labradoodles develop into sociable, self-assured dogs, socialization is equally crucial. Early socialization with a variety of places, people, and animals aids in the development of positive social skills and lessens the possibility of later fear or hostility. Playdates, puppy lessons, and frequent visits to parks may all help socialize your dog.

To properly teach and socialize Australian Labradoodles, consistency, patience, and positive reinforcement are essential. These adorable canines have the potential to develop into well-adjusted, content family members with the right training and care.

Basic Instructions For An Australian Labradoodle

Australian Labradoodles are well-behaved, trainable, and clever dogs. The following fundamental instructions are crucial for their instruction:

1. Holding a goodie close to your Labradoodle's nose and gradually pushing it higher will teach them to sit when asked to do so. Their bottom will automatically descend into a sitting posture as their head

rises. When they sit, pamper them and give them praise.

2. Teach your Labradoodle to remain put until you instruct them to release them. Start by having them sit, then say "stay," put your open palm in front of their face, and take a step back. If they maintain their posture, give them praise and rewards. Increase the length and distance gradually.

3. Lie Down: Begin by having your Labradoodle sit before teaching them how to lie down. A treat should be held in front of their nose and then moved carefully to the ground. Their body will naturally drop into a laying posture as they proceed with the

goodie. When they lay down, give them praise and rewards.

4. Teach your Labradoodle to come to you by calling him or her. Start in a private, confined space and cheerfully call their name followed by the word "come". Give them rewards and compliments when they approach you. Increase the distance gradually and practice in various settings.

When training your Australian Labradoodle, consistency, patience, and positive reinforcement are essential. To sustain their attention and enthusiasm, make training sessions brief and engaging.

Working Breed Of The Australian Labradoodle

The Australian Labradoodle is a multipurpose and clever breed that does well as both a family companion and a working dog. This breed, which was developed in Australia, mixes characteristics from the Labrador Retriever, Poodle, and other breeds to produce a canine with exceptional skills.

Australian Labradoodles are often used as therapy dogs, search and rescue dogs, and support dogs for people with impairments in the workplace. They are perfect for these positions because of their amiable disposition, hypoallergenic coat, and great trainability. They have an intuitive sense of empathy and a great desire to please their handlers, which enable them to be excellent comforters and helpers.

Australian Labradoodles may be taught for a variety of jobs thanks to their intelligence and agility, including obedience contests, agility trials, and even serving as guide dogs for the blind.

They excel at jobs like recovering game or working in water-based areas because of their innate retrieving instincts and love of the water.

Australian Labradoodles have established themselves as dependable and valued working dogs in a variety of professional contexts because of their remarkable work ethic, versatility, and mild demeanor.

CHAPTER SIX

As A Family Pet:
Australian Labradoodle

Families looking for a devoted and social companion should strongly consider getting an Australian Labradoodle. This breed has become well-liked as a great family pet because of its pleasant demeanor, intelligence, and low-shedding coat.

The remarkable temperament of the Australian Labradoodle is one of its most important qualities. These dogs are renowned for being kind and tolerant, which makes them wonderful pets for kids of all ages. They like participating in family activities, whether it be playing in the garden or snuggling on the sofa and are quite friendly.

Australian Labradoodles are also extremely trainable due to their intelligence and desire to please. They pick up simple obedience cues quickly and may be further taught to do more difficult jobs and stunts.

They can easily adapt to a variety of living arrangements, including flats or homes with extensive yards, thanks to this breed's intelligence.

The non-shedding, hypoallergenic coat of the Australian Labradoodle is another benefit. They are thus a great option for households with allergy sufferers since they release fewer allergens and shed less often.

To keep their coat healthy, regular grooming is required, but it is a little price to pay for a companion that gives so much happiness and pleasure.

The Australian Labradoodle is a wonderful family companion because of its intelligent, amiable nature, and low-shedding coat. They are a wonderful option for families looking for a devoted and caring four-legged addition to their home since they love human company and get along well with kids.

Compatibility Of The Australian Labradoodle Dog With Kids And Other Animals

The Australian Labradoodle is renowned for being amiable and kind, making it a breed that gets along well with families that have kids and other pets.

These dogs are excellent companions for children of all ages because of their well-known sociable and friendly disposition. Australian Labradoodles often exhibit tolerance and patience, which is important when socializing with young children. They naturally have a softness and protectiveness for children, which makes them good playmates. Since they are gregarious and energetic, they can keep up with kids' high levels of energy while engaging in a variety of games and activities.

Australian Labradoodles often get along well with other animals, making them a good choice for households with other pets.

They may establish friendly connections with cats, other dogs, and even smaller animals like rabbits or guinea pigs because of their sociable and friendly nature. For the Labradoodle and other pets to get along, early socialization and appropriate introductions are crucial.

Because each dog's temperament may differ, its compatibility with kids and other animals depends on the particular dog's personality and training. To keep the environment safe and peaceful for everyone, responsible ownership, monitoring, and educating kids on how to treat dogs with respect are essential.

In conclusion, the Australian Labradoodle is a very suitable breed for families looking for a furry buddy that can flourish in a multi-pet home because of their friendly and laid-back personality as well as their affection for kids and other pets.

Australian Labradoodle Dog Breeding And Reproduction

A well-liked and endearing breed, the Australian Labradoodle is renowned for its wit, devotion, and hypoallergenic coat.

To preserve the breed's intended features and qualities, breeding and reproduction in Australian Labradoodles need careful selection and managed breeding techniques.

Selecting acceptable parent dogs that fulfill particular health, temperament, and conformation requirements is usually the first step in breeding Australian Labradoodles. To reduce the danger of hereditary disorders, ethical breeders pay particular attention to genetic health testing. To suit the tastes of future owners, they could also take into account characteristics like coat type, size, and color.

To breed a female Labradoodle, one must first wait until she is in heat, which is a time when she is most amenable to mating. Breeders keep a close eye on the female's cycle and may utilize hormone tests or behavioral indicators to decide when is the best time to procreate.

An appropriate stud dog is then mated with the female to create a balanced and varied genetic mix.

The female goes through an approximately 63-day gestation phase after a successful mating. Breeders make sure the mother and growing pups are healthy and happy throughout this period by giving them the right food, exercise, and medical attention.

To encourage the pups' physical and mental growth after birth, they need regular attention and socializing. To guarantee well-rounded and self-assured adult dogs, breeders often use early neurological stimulation approaches and progressively expose them to a variety of stimuli and surroundings.

In conclusion, careful parent dog selection, attention to genetic health testing, and ethical breeding procedures are all important aspects of Australian Labradoodle breeding and reproduction.

The objective is to raise happy, healthy pups that exhibit the breed's desirable characteristics and become excellent companions for their future owners.

CHAPTER SEVEN
The Commitment To And Responsible Ownership Of An Australian Labradoodle Dog

When it comes to Australian Labradoodle dogs, responsible ownership and dedication are essential. To flourish, these witty and gregarious canines need the right love, care, and attention.

Owners that are responsible make sure their Labradoodles get routine veterinarian care, like shots, checkups, and grooming. To keep their dogs healthy and happy, they provide them with a balanced diet, plenty of exercise, and mental stimulation. Responsible pet owners also place a high priority on socialization and training to raise dogs who are well-mannered and submissive. They are dedicated to reducing overbreeding and recognize the value of spaying and neutering. Responsible pet care also entails creating a warm, secure atmosphere where the Labradoodle may thrive as a beloved part of the family.

Breeding Considerations And Procedures For Australian Labradoodle Dogs

To guarantee healthy and attractive offspring, the breeding procedure and considerations for Australian Labradoodle dogs take several key elements into account. Labradoodles and Poodles, as well as other breeds including the Irish Water Spaniel and English Cocker Spaniel, are used to create Australian Labradoodles.

First and foremost, ethical breeders choose parent dogs carefully for their temperament, health, and genetic heritage. To find any genetic problems and stop them from being passed on to future generations, health screenings are essential. Exams of the eyes, hips, and elbows as well as DNA testing for hereditary abnormalities are a few examples of these exams.

Breeders then take the required features into account, such as size (standard, medium, or miniature), coat type (hair, fleece, or wool), and color variations. With selective breeding, breed traits like intelligence, a pleasant disposition, and a hypoallergenic coat are kept constant.

Breeding couples are selected based on genetic variety and

qualities that complement one another. The safety and welfare of the participating dogs are ensured by careful observation of the mating procedure.

To produce healthy and appealing pups while keeping the breed's distinctive characteristics, the breeding procedure for Australian Labradoodles often includes painstaking selection, health testing, and careful evaluation of attributes.

Breeders that practice responsible breeding put the well-being of their dogs first and work to enhance the breed with each new generation.

How to Choose a Reliable Breeder for an Australian Labradoodle

There are a few key things to take into account when choosing a reliable breeder for an Australian Labradoodle. Make sure the breeder, first and foremost, has a good standing in the dog breeding world. Seek breeders that have memberships in respected organizations like the International Australian Labradoodle Association or the Australian Labradoodle Association.

A trustworthy breeder will put their pets' health and welfare first. They will carry out accurate health examinations to check for hereditary illnesses and provide you with the required paperwork. They will also be familiar with the particular traits, temperament, and grooming requirements of the breed.

It is very advised to visit the breeder's facilities. This will enable you to check on the dogs' living arrangements and make sure they are tidy, cared for, and given enough room.

A trustworthy breeder would be delighted to respond to your inquiries and provide you with details about the dog's pedigree and any health assurances they make available.

Keep in mind that trustworthy breeders place a high priority on the well-being of their dogs and will inquire about your ability to provide them with an appropriate and loving home. You'll have a far better chance of taking home a healthy, well-socialized Australian Labradoodle if you take the time to select a reputable breeder.

CHAPTER EIGHT

The Australian Labradoodle Dog's Pregnancy And Whelping

Like with any dog breed, the Australian Labradoodle's pregnancy and whelping period are both thrilling and important. For Labradoodles, the usual gestation time is 58 to 68 days.

It's crucial to provide the pregnant dog with a healthy diet, frequent checkups with the doctor, and a tranquil, comfortable environment throughout this time.

The female Labradoodle may engage in nesting activities, get agitated, and demonstrate a reduction in appetite as the due date draws near. It is best to set up a whelping space with cozy bedding and a peaceful environment for her to give birth. Although there might be exceptions, labradoodle litter sizes normally vary from 6 to 8 pups.

The female pushes and delivers each youngster throughout the several-hour-long whelping procedure. Although it is essential to provide support and aid when required, interference should be kept to a minimum to enable the natural process to take place.

The mother will naturally clean and feed the pups as soon as they are born. It's crucial to keep a careful eye on the pups to make sure they are properly feeding and gaining weight. To ensure the health and well-being of both the mother and her pups throughout the postnatal period, regular veterinarian examinations and appropriate treatment are crucial.

The Typical Australian Labradoodle Dog's Life Expectancy

An Australian Labradoodle dog may live for 12 to 15 years on average. It is crucial to remember that this estimate might change depending on several variables, including genetics, general health, nutrition, activity, and the quality of veterinarian care given.

Compared to several other dog breeds, Australian Labradoodles are known to have rather lengthy lives. This is due to their mixed lineage, which includes Labradors, Poodles, and other breeds chosen for their advantageous characteristics.

The goal is to improve the overall genetic variety and decrease the probability of acquiring certain breed-specific health problems.

An Australian Labradoodle needs a good diet, frequent exercise, regular veterinarian checkups, and a secure, stimulating environment to live a longer, healthier life. They may live longer and be healthier if they practice proper oral hygiene, manage their weight, get their shots, and get preventative treatments on time.

Australian Labradoodle Dog's Conclusion

In conclusion, the Australian Labradoodle is a magnificent canine variety that has won the hearts of many canine lovers all over the globe.

This breed has become a cherished companion for families, individuals, and even those in need of therapy or assistance dogs because of its exceptional blend of intellect, trainability, and friendly disposition.

The goal to develop a low-shedding, hypoallergenic service dog with a pleasant disposition gave rise to the Australian Labradoodle.

These dogs have achieved not just those original objectives but have also beyond expectations in terms of their general health, adaptability, and flexibility via careful breeding and selection.

These canines have excelled in several capacities, including rehabilitation work, search and rescue, and service as guide dogs for the blind. They like interacting with people, are well-regarded for being perceptive, and have a strong connection to their owners.

It's simple to see why the popularity of the Australian Labradoodle is growing.

They are a fantastic addition to any household or community because of their endearing personalities, spectacular features, and amazing skills.

Whether you're looking for a lifelong buddy, a coworker, or just a devoted companion, the Australian Labradoodle is certain to brighten your day with happiness, love, and infinite experiences.